Progressive Usui Reiki

Level 1

Tammie L Hada

CONTENTS

SECTION 1

OVERVIEW OF REIKI

ABOUT THE AUTHOR

Welcome to Energy for Wellness: Level I Reiki Course. My name is Tammie and I am a Reiki Master that has been practicing for over ten years. I am also certified in Pranic Healing, Angels & Spirit Guides, Higher Soul, Crystal Healing, and my latest certification is in Spiritual Counseling. I also practice extensive breathe work, meditation and Qi Gong/Tai Chi. In addition to these I do hold a traditional B.S. in Instructional Media & Technology as well as a M.S. in Psychology.

As a lightworker, I am grateful to be in service to humanity in anyway that I can, and I don't believe in coincidences. Whether you purchased this manual online or are enrolled in my class, I suspect that you are because you too have received the call; whether  you realize it consciously yet or not. Helping those to feel better in anyway is a classic sign for many. Don't be surprised if you even feel like you know your classmates from somewhere but you just can't place them. Enjoy the Deja vu and other synchronicities that you may experience. On that note, welcome again! I am delighted to have you in class! Let's begin with a brief description of Reiki.

BRIEF DESCRIPTION

"Rei" means universal. "Ki" means life force. Reiki can be pronounced Rye-key or Ray-key or Ree-key. The original pronunciation is Rye-key. You might catch me saying all three from time to time. My Master pronounced it Ray-key and that is what I try to stick with. It is a form of Eastern energy healing that has been used for many thousands of years. In Christianity, it is referred to as "the laying on of hands." In modern nursing, it is referred to as "Therapeutic Touch." It is basically healing at the energetic level. The main differences between them is the attunements given in Reiki. Truly anyone can practice energy healing, however; the attunement process considerably amplifies the abilities of the practitioner and it becomes palpable. Especially when your client is very open and receptive to drawing the Reiki from you.

HISTORY AND ORIGINS

In the beginning, Reiki was taught verbally only. It was only when Grand Master Mikao Usui put the processes in writing to share with the world in the mid nineteenth century. There are so many different forms of Reiki that have surfaced over the recent years, our focus is on the most powerful and original—Usui Reiki.

CHARACTERISTICS

What makes this course progressive are the specific methods and techniques I teach based on my knowledge of energy and the body. The activation of important chakras and breathe work are a couple of examples. Life force energy in Reiki is known in most cultures. Where Ki is Japanese for life force, it is Chi/Qi in Chinese, and it is known as Prana in India.

The human body has several energetic layers contained in what's called an aura. It is inside the aura that our chakras are located. Traditional Usui Reiki and all others concentrate on the 7 main chakras, where here in *Progressive* Usui Reiki we will be covering 11 minimum. There are in fact many more. Chakras are the body's energy centers and they operate similar to the way the brain controls the body through the nerve signals it sends. There is a chakra for each section of the body that controls those respective organs. A complete diagram of these chakras is included in Section 3 of this manual.

When these energy centers and the aura itself are dirty or weak, it allows the body to easily become unwell. By cleansing the chakras and the aura, clients almost instantly become rejuvenated. Reiki energy offers continuous healing; it continues to work from 24-72 hours after a treatment. Most clients state they continually felt better over the course of a couple days. The specific hand placements then further the healing by treating ailments known and unknown to the clients.
It is also important to note the characteristics that make the body unwell, or what can make our aura dirty and slow down or weaken our chakras. Drugs and alcohol, fast food, un-natural processed foods, anxiety, poor sleep, and negative thoughts. Our beliefs, thoughts, and emotions

actually do create our realities. I cannot stress enough to change the voice inside your head to be kind and loving to yourself and others—always. While this isn't a course on manifesting, changing your thoughts, beliefs, and emotions will help you succeed at everything you do or try to obtain and keep you healthy!
Research in the medical field has explained extensively how and why placebos work. Changing your internal chatter works much in the same way as the placebo effect. Life really is what you make it, so think, feel, and believe that it is good!

Finally, Reiki's main function is to heal and to facilitate the body's natural healing modalities. By using Reiki methods, you are holistically treating the whole mind, body, and spirit for continued health. When your life force energy is high, you have the ability to handle life's twists with ease, and you will not fall ill as often. Next, the 5 Reiki principles will be outlined for you. These are daily affirmations that help to keep us positive and authentic.

FIVE REIKI PRINCIPLES

Just for today, I will not worry.
Just for today, I will not be angry.
Just for today, I will do my work honestly.
Just for today, I will be grateful for my many blessings.
Just for today, I will be kind to my neighbor
and every living thing.

The beauty of these affirmations is if you have a particularly rough day, tomorrow is always another day to start again! These five principles are only a guide to help us stay grounded on what's important in life. You may feel called to change or replace one or more and that is just fine. What is important is that you use what resonates with you on a personal level.

LEARNING OBJECTIVES

You will learn:
1. How to activate specific chakras
2. Specific breathing techniques to aid in energy flow
3. The placements for fine-point targeting and broader spectrum healing using your hands and fingers
4. Aura and Chakra scanning and cleansing
5. Tips for raising your own vibrational frequencies and those of your clients.
6. How to develop and train your intuition to guide your energy flow.

In addition, you will be specifically attuned as a level I practitioner after successfully completing the course. Attunements raise your energy level as a conductor as much 80-90%! (In class participants only.)

Author's Note-
If you purchased this manual online and did not take a class with me, I want to congratulate you for taking that first step into the unknown. You are a brave soul! Continue seeking your truth. While Reiki can be done by anyone willing to be a conduit for life force energy, I feel it is im-

portant you should know that being attuned will make a huge difference for your practice.

I recommend you find a Reiki master in your area that would be willing to attune you. They may in fact want to test your knowledge to be sure you are ready to be attuned. So prepare yourself and practice, practice, practice! I firmly believe that when attuned properly, it can boost your abilities by over 80%! You may find a Reiki master who insists you take his/her class before attunements will be given. Attunements are to be taken very seriously, however; if you feel you are ready (you know in your heart of hearts) then keep looking! If for whatever reason you do not want to repeat the class then you will find another master who is willing. Just be open and receptive. Namaste!

SECTION 2

INITIAL PREPARATION
GROUNDING

Grounding yourself is very important. When we are grounded, the Reiki flows through us like we're the perfect conduit. There are several ways in which to ground. Walking in nature, wearing crystals, and meditation/visualizations. When walking in nature, be barefoot if possible. If not, sit or stand by a tree and place both hands on the tree, or even hug the tree in appreciation of the essential oxygen it puts out for us and its beauty. Spend at least ten minutes with your tree. You should also stop to smell the flowers in appreciation of their scent and beauty. Touch the stem and petals, appreciate the softness of nature.

In addition, take time to listen to the birds and the wind while you are grounding. Be in the present moment. Pay attention to your breath. Feel it enter through your nostrils. Feel your lower abdomen inflate on every inhale. Feel it deflate on every exhale and feel it exit your nose. This will help you stay in the present moment and enjoy nature to its fullest and perfectly ground you at the same time.

Crystals are a great way to keep yourself grounded. There are many that work very well. In my opinion, the two strongest are Hematite and Smokey Quartz. There is also Black Tourmaline, Jasper, and Shungite to name a few 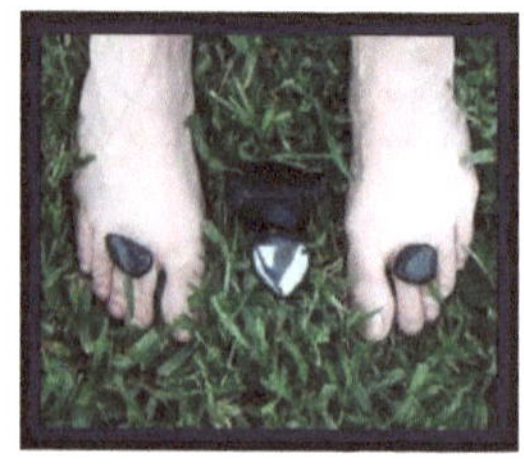 more. I recommend going in person and testing the crystals before you make your final purchase. Many herbal shops carry a variety of crystals now. It's important the crystals you choose work well for you. You will know this immediately upon picking up the crystal. You will feel its vibration in your hand. In time your ability to feel these vibrations will get even stronger. I use the soft pads of my finger tips to feel for the vibrations.

Yet another way to get yourself grounded is to sit comfortably on the floor or ground. Then visualize your feet (and if you like your legs up to your knees, whatever you are comfortable with) growing down into mother earth like long roots.

Visualize your roots going miles deep into the earth. Hold this sturdy feeling for at least ten minutes. This type of grounding can be just as effective as actually being out in nature.

I recommend to ground yourself as often as you feel necessary. The more grounded you are, the healthier and stronger you will feel. Clarity of the mind, heightened senses, and intuition are also nice benefits of grounding.

BREATHING

As previously mentioned, focusing on your breath is an excellent way to stay in the present moment. This is key for peace in your mind and heart. Paying attention to how it feels as you breathe in. Feel it enter and leave your nose, feel your abdomen extend and retract. After a few breaths, you are ready for a more advanced technique.

Sit with an erect spine but relaxed shoulders. It is important for your chakras to align. Relax your perineum and breathe in and out deep through your nose visualizing the energy in the air entering your crown chakra and earth energy entering in through the root chakra. The perineum is the space between the anus and vagina in women. It is between the testicles and anus in men. With practice you will feel these two chakras "waking up." Now visualize this energy being stored in your energy center, about an inch or so down from your navel. Continue breathing steadily in an out your nose about 10 times, storing up this energy. You may visualize the energy that comes in through the root chakra going into your reserves and the energy coming down from your crown going into your heart chakra. You may feel your heart chakra opening, intense love and compassion lives here. This is ideal for beginning a Reiki session.

Breathing steadily in and out through your nose using this visualization is exactly what you will be doing during a session. However, instead of storing the energy or directing it to your heart; you will feel it leaving your hand and finger chakras.

ACTIVATE HAND & FINGER CHAKRAS

To activate your hand chakras, press firmly into the palm of your right hand using your left thumb. Press in and hold for about two seconds. Do the same with your left hand and right thumb. Then you want to stretch your hand out, bending the fingers back as far as they will go on their own.

Then, as if to say "I love you this much," stretch your hands out to the sides and up —this stretches the tendons and muscles in your arms (while keeping your hands  stretched open as well). While feeling the pull in your arms, you should feel a sensation in the palms of your hands. Now bring the palms of your hands close together to feel the energy in your hands. Repeat until you feel the sensations. You may repeat this exercise daily until your palms stay open and active for you.

To activate your finger chakras, firmly pinch each fingertip pad with the opposite hand. Then open and close your hand vigorously about ten times. You may repeat this process just as often as you do your palms. Your hands are now ready for the flow of energy through them. In just a bit, we will cover what positions to hold your hands and fingers in during treatments. It is also good practice to activate both your hands and fingertips before each healing session in the beginning. Soon you won't need to reactivate, unless you are not as grounded as you typically are.

HYDRATE AND CLEANSE

Hydrating your body is important for energy flow and to prevent headaches from dehydration. Many people have remarked they have gotten headaches after completing several treatments without hydrating in between. I recommend a glass of spring water, (or filtered water with the impurities removed, i.e., chlorine and fluoride) before and after your treatment sessions.

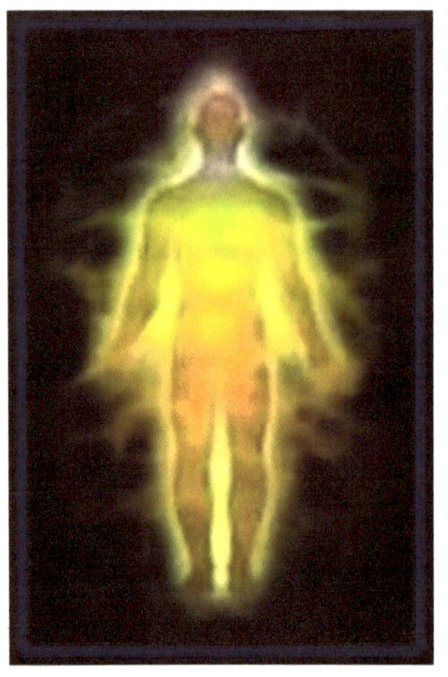

In addition to hydrating, cleaning your own aura and the room you are working in is also highly recommended. Activate hand and finger chakras and sweep your cupped, dominant hand (palm in) from head (crown) to root (groin) about five times.

After cleansing your aura, cleanse the room you will be working in from any residual energy that may be lingering.

You can use sage or incense, carefully; or if you prefer a non smoke method, there are various recipes online for cleansing your sacred space. Many use a blend of lemon essential oil, rose essential oil, bits of white sage and mixed with spring water.

Then you just mist the room down and sweep your hands moving the stagnant energy out an open window. You may also use visualizations. I visualize a bright white light that fills the room and instantly raises the vibrations and cleanses the room. Then I put a large bowl of spring water and sea salt (using about two cups sea salt to four quart bowl of water). This bowl acts as a negativity magnet. While your working on your client, any negativities you remove from them will be absorbed by that bowl. You may already have your own methods different from the aforementioned ways, and that's a good thing! Use what resonates with you.

Also, the first step on your client should be to cleanse their aura. After activating hand and finger chakras again, I usually do an invocation. That will be discussed in detail in the *Reiki in Action* (Section 3) of this manual. After your invocation or prayer, you can then use your dominant hand to sweep your clients aura from head to toe. Moving at a steady pace with hand cupped slightly, you are scooping away anything that shouldn't be there. The more you use your Reiki, the more familiar with auras you will become. Your hands will become super sensitive to cold spots, hot spots, even an odd tingling sensations where your attention is needed. If after you cleanse their aura, (during the scan) you still feel those places, those are areas that will need your attention after you've finished with their chakra cleansing.

Use the aura cleansing time to also scan carefully their entire body. Pay close attention to what you feel with your hands. This will help your hands become more sensitive and it will help you become aware of your cli-

ent's ailments, some of which may not be apparent to them. I will usually scan my clients first to get a grasp on their needs and then discuss with them whatever they want to address. Then, I compare with what I noticed during the scan. In time you will be able to anticipate their needs and you will be spot on! However, it is always good practice to ask even though, you may already know. It is very important that your client feels they are being heard and understood. It is also highly advisable to have your client drink a glass of spring water before leaving you. Flushing of toxins is very important. Be sure they drink at least eight 8oz glasses of water every day for the next three days. If they can tolerate more, or their normal consumption is more, that works beautifully too! The next section discusses further, the possible reactions that clients may or may not experience.

WARNINGS AND INTERACTIONS

On occasion a client may complain that they are feeling worse after a treatment. This is because the Reiki energy is bringing to the surface all the toxins that need to be released and drinking plenty of water is imperative. Also, the energy sessions should be closer together for those clients who experience a reaction. With any kind of reaction, increasing the frequency of the treatments will not only provide your client with much needed relief, but will speed his/her healing. It is good practice to inform your client of these in advance of their treatment.

Do not treat people with pacemakers. The energy can alter the rhythm. Similarly, if you choose to treat someone with diabetes, you must inform your client that they will require less insulin and must check their glucose levels before every intended dose. Other reactions include itchiness, emotional responses, achiness, fatigue, flu-like

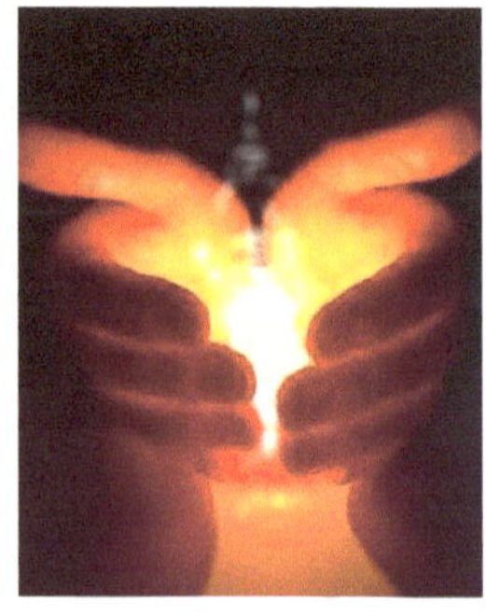

symptoms, or brain fog. Some clients have reported memory flashes that trigger the emotional responses.

With emotional responses and memory flashes, these could be old wounds that have resurfaced so your client can address them and let them go. Invoking the violet flame in meditation will help your client forgive all involved including his/herself. When we have old hurts that we have repressed, they will manifest as chronic pain in various areas of the body. Reiki can heal the physical pain to the point the old hurt rises to the surface, but at that time your client must do his/her part to release.

The violet flame meditation can be invoked by you and your client. Have them do this mediation while you complete their treatment. While they are lying down, receiving their treatment, have them repeat these words over and over again. "I am a being of the violet fire. I am the purity God desires." While they are repeating this mantra, they should visualize violet flames engulfing their body and healing all traumas, known and unknown with forgiveness in his/her heart.

This meditation is very effective and you as the practitioner can also invoke the violet flame by visualizing the violet flames coming out of your hands with your Reiki energy. This will speed the healing of your client. You can say the mantra silently, while your client speaks it aloud. If you or your client prefers, the word "source" or "universe" can be used in place of God. Always work with your own intuition and client preference.

SECTION 3

REIKI IN ACTION
BENEFITS OF REIKI

A complete Reiki treatment will include the clearing and opening of all chakras, which will in turn balance the life force energy within your client. This initiates the bodies natural healing abilities. Any toxins present in the body will be loosened to be flushed out by your client's urinary and lymph systems. When we cleanse and balance our systems, this gives our entire immune system a boost of fresh energy to fight off all illnesses and improves our outlook on life in general. The benefits of Reiki include but are not limited to the following:

Destress, relaxation, better sleep, relieves pain

Clears brain fog, increased focus, better overall mood

Renewed energy levels, raises vibrational frequencies

Gradual healing of chronic conditions, overall improved health

Detoxifies, dissolves energy blockages, releases emotions

See the section entitled, "Self Treatments and Hand Positions" for a diagram of the Chakra System. You will come to know these well.

In addition to these benefits, you and your clients will notice the desire for healthier living. Eating habits may change with the desire for organic or healthier food choices. Household products may change to all natural.

Many begin Tai Chi/Qi Gung or Yoga. These desires for healthier living are all very natural and I urge you to go with whatever resonates with you.

While the benefits of Reiki have been documented many times over, some wonder if it can actually be seen. In some healing modalities the use of color is involved. For example, green is used for cleansing. The practitioner would visualize green flowing energy from their hands or crystals when treating. Most of these practitioners are able to see this energy. As far as other means to see it, *Kirlian Photography* is an excellent method to see Reiki in action. This method also captures the person's aura. I recommend getting this done if ever you are at an expo where it's been offered. The Body, Mind, and Spirit Expo comes to the Chicago area every March and Tinley Park every June. These expos almost always offer some form of this technology.

BEFORE YOU BEGIN

As previously mentioned in the *Initial Preparation* (section 1), there are several things to do before you begin a treatment. Living well, including self treatments, is very important from a practitioner view point. Keeping your self grounded, hydrated, and your aura cleansed just before a session are the perfect conditions for a successful treatment and a pleased client. Breathing during a session is also very important for the energy flow. Below is a specific technique for you to practice.

Breathing techniques are designed to assist the body to relax. When we breathe through the mouth we allow impurities to enter our body freely.is found in all living things and is considered to be the active principle or vitality of life itself.meditation for example,breathing floods the body with the extra energy and oxygen,helps to calm and still the mind. It is important to keep an even rhythm between inhalation and exhalation in order to maintain the balance of the energy  flowing in and through you.Breathing in and out through the nose is most effective.

The first breathing exercise is the 6-3-6 Breath. Practicing this type of breathing during meditation will help you master it quickly. This technique can be used for storing energy as well as giving a treatment.

You will breathe in for a count of six, hold for a count of three, breathe out for another count of six, and repeat.

With visualizations for storing energy: With a relaxed perineum, breath in through the nose for a count of six. While you breathe in, visualize the energy coming up from your root or sex chakra as well as down from your crown chakra. If you are standing, visualize the energy coming up from your feet chakras instead. Visualize the energy coming up from the root/sex or feet chakras and upon holding for the count of three, visualize it arriving at your storage reservoir which is located about an inch and a half below your navel. Breathing out for a count of six, visualizing the energy actually entering your storage reservoir. Repeat the breath in for a count of six, pulling in the energy, while holding for three, it arrives at your reservoir, and then breathing out for a count of six actually moves it into your reservoir.

The storage aspect can be done before your client arrives. During the actual treatment, you will visualize all the energy going through your heart chakra and then out your hand and finger chakras. Once this is mastered you may incorporate a visualization of something or someone you love dearly to activate your heart chakra and give your energy flow a significant boost.

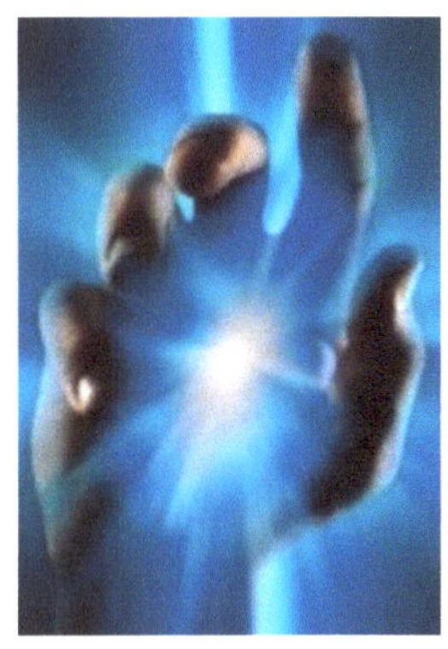

With visualizations for treatments: Breathing in for a count of six, visualize the energy coming down from the crown chakra flowing towards your heart chakra. The energy coming up from your feet chakras is heading towards your heart chakra as well. Upon holding for a count of three the energy reaches and enters your heart chakra. Breathing out for a count of six moves the energy from your heart chakra down your arms and out your hand chakras.

Now is a good time to activate your hand and finger chakras (refer back to section 2, entitled, "Activate Hand and Finger Chakras"). The next step is simply to vigorously rub the palms of your hands together generating friction and further opening your hand chakras. The steps in detail will be outlined in the section called Treatments for Others & Hand Positions.

Before cleansing your client's aura and scanning them which would come next, you would say your prayer or invocation. This will be discussed in detail on the next page. See the previous Section (2), Hydrate & Cleanse in this manual for details on auras and scanning. In addition, offering your client water prior to beginning is also important. Proper hydration is crucial and before they arrive they should be told to have already drank a few glasses of spring water.

INVOKATION/PRAYER

I stress the importance of asking for help because we are not the healers. We are merely the conduits of this life force energy. It flows through us and is absorbed by our clients. Whether you believe in angels, God, or any other higher power, it is important to ask for help. If you are not spiritual or religious in any way, you may simply refer to the higher power as the universe or whatever resonates with you. Below is a couple of examples of how to invoke the divine to assist you.

Example 1: Put your hands in prayer position inside your heart chakra (up close to your chest). This is the

Gassho position. Say the following: "I call upon the first Reiki Masters and to all healing angels for guidance and assistance. Please let the Reiki flow. Please let the Reiki flow. Please let the Reiki flow." (Three times with sincerity.)

Example 2: Hold your hands out at waist level, palms up and open. Say the following: "I call upon the Holy Mother, Holy Father, and all healing angels to guide and assist me in the highest healing possible for (insert name of client). Please let the Reiki flow. Please let the Reiki flow. Please let the Reiki flow." If either of these invocations/prayers do not resonate with you, feel free to devise your own personal

invocation or prayer.

In the beginning, it is a good idea to keep the chatter to a minimum while performing a session. Stay focused and concentrate on your breath, hand movements, and what sensations you are feeling. Stay in the moment. Feel free to hold your hands in whatever position resonates with you. There is no right or wrong way to the invocation or prayer as long as you say, "Please, let the Reiki flow," three times. Saying it three times is—in a way, activating your Reiki. You can reverse it and say, "Let the Reiki flow please," as long as you ask three times. My Reiki flows much stronger when I ask for divine assistance and yours will too. You may even feel your hands being guided by the healing angels. That always gets my Reiki flowing strong as well and gives me a nice "ah-ha" moment!

HAND POSES

The three most important hand poses are depicted in these graphics to the right. The 5-finger laser point, 2-finger fine point, and gently cupped hand.

Using your intuition, you will know when to switch from the cupped hands position to a more focused energy. Small areas on the surface or even small areas that are deep in the body are examples of when to use focused Reiki.

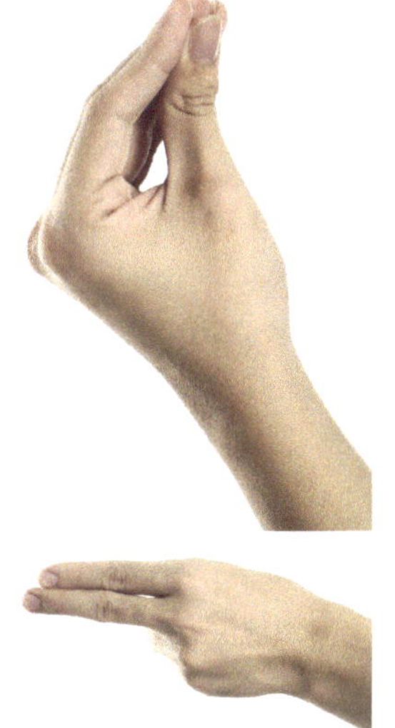

The focused energy hand poses are the reason for activating the finger chakras. Also, it is noteworthy that touching is not required to give Reiki energy treatments. If your intuition tells you to touch, be sure to ask permission first.

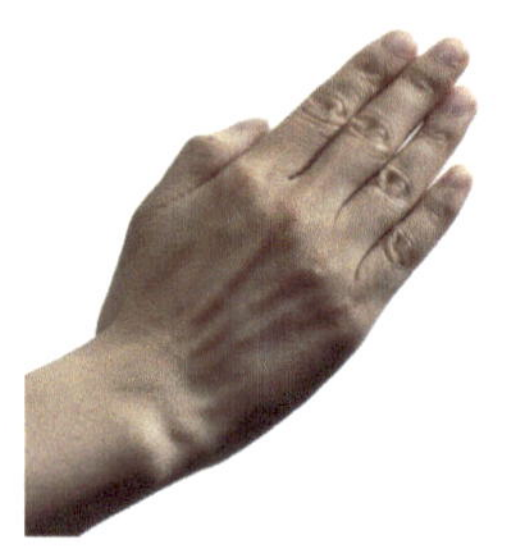

SELF-TREATMENTS AND HAND POSITIONS

After you have completed all the initial steps, perform the invocation and begin your breathing. First cleans your aura then place your gently cupped hands on each chakra (it's okay if you cannot reach them all, **Reiki energy flows where your attention goes**. Just place your hands near the intended chakra and think of that chakra. Reiki will go there automatically. Length of time for each one varies. Use your intuition, or let 3-5 minutes on each is a good standard. On the next page is a diagram of the chakra placement. After you complete the chakras you can move on to the specific Reiki hand positions. They are shown below.

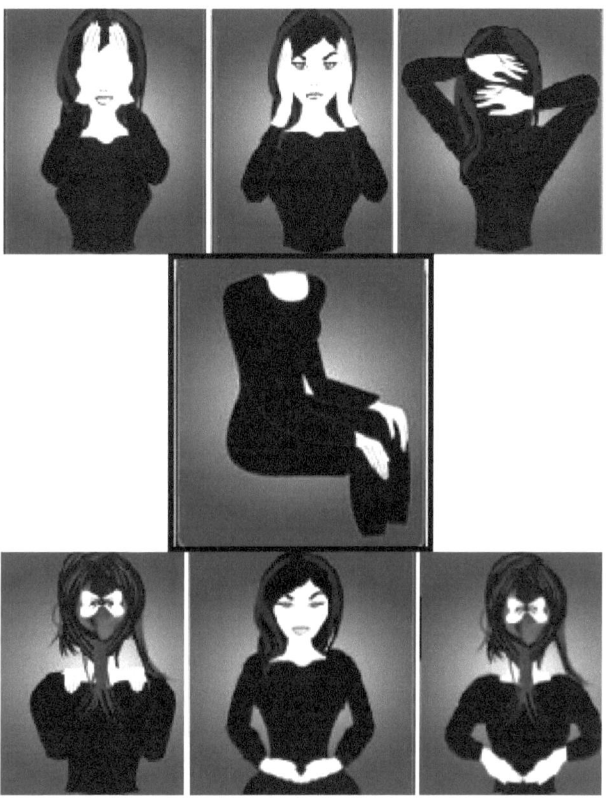

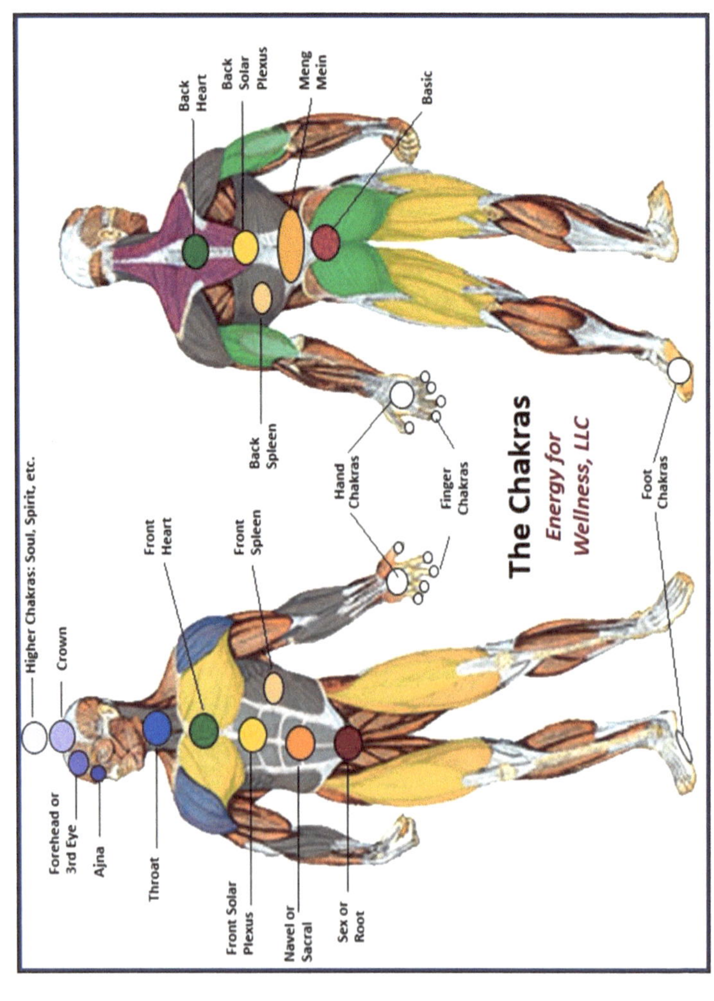
Back Heart
Back Solar Plexus
Meng Mein
Basic
Back Spleen
Hand Chakras
Finger Chakras
Foot Chakras
Higher Chakras: Soul, Spirit, etc.
Crown
Forehead or 3rd Eye
Ajna
Throat
Front Heart
Front Spleen
Front Solar Plexus
Navel or Sacral
Sex or Root
The Chakras
Energy for Wellness, LLC

TREATMENTS FOR OTHERS AND HAND POSITIONS

After you have completed all the initial steps, perform the invocation and begin your breathing. First cleans their aura and scan. Take notice of all sensations you may feel. Make a mental note of anything you notice to go back to after the chakras are finished.   Then place your gently cupped hands on each chakra doing the front of their body first. (Refer back to the diagram of the chakra placement as often as you wish.) Each placement should take 3-5 minutes, depending on your intuition and their body language. If you notice a twitch for example in the area you are treating, that signifies it's time to move on to the next area. After the chakras are completed on their front side, continue with the regular Reiki hand placements for the front side. Then address any special areas you noticed during the scan. Once the front side is complete, have your client flip over to resume the chakras on the back side, and then continue with the regular Reiki hand positions. The Reiki hand positions are below.

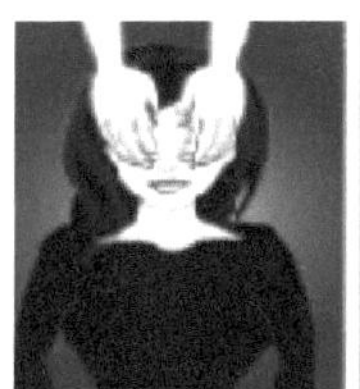

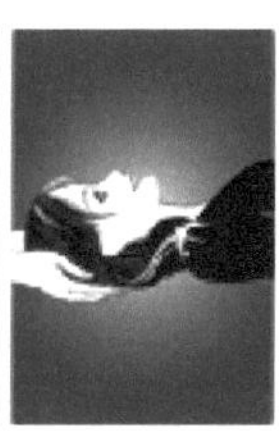

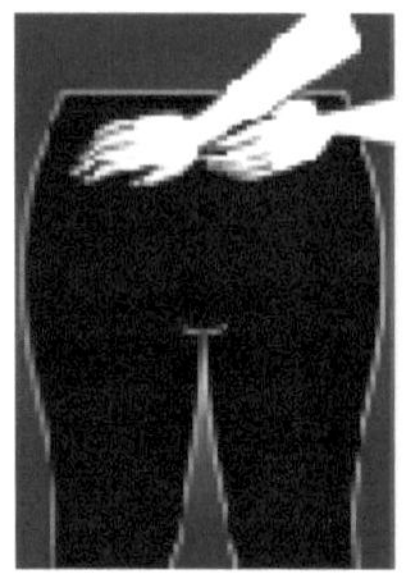 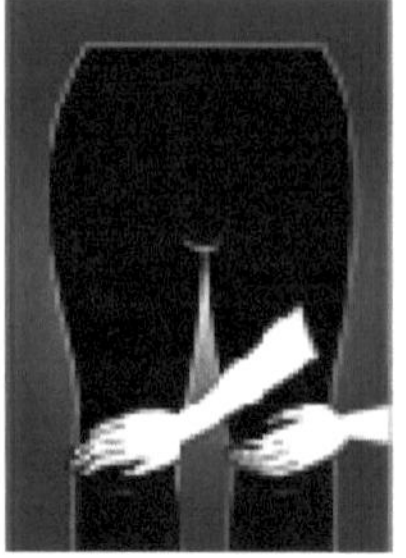 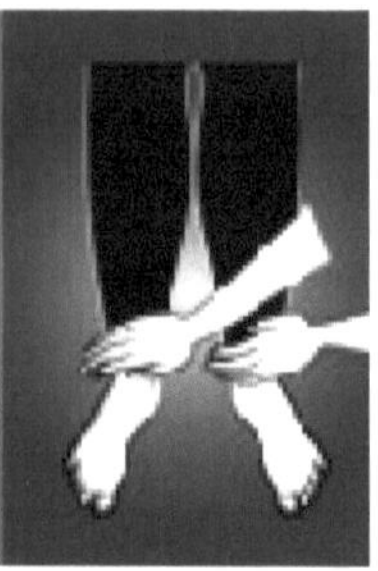

Below are all the steps in the order in which they are to be performed. Use these as a general guide. I suggest they be followed in the beginning of your practice until you develop your own system that resonates with you. It is very possible that in time you will discover many things that work better for you. Always follow your intuition.

Steps for quick reference on treating others:

1. Ground and hydrate yourself, (Covered in Section-2) Walking in nature, wearing crystals, and/or meditation/ visualizations; drinking at least one glass of spring water.

2. Breathing for energy storage, (Covered in Section-2) Relax your perineum and breathe in and out deep through your nose visualizing the energy in the air entering your crown chakra and earth energy entering in through the root chakra. Now visualize this energy being stored in your energy center, about an inch or so down from your navel.

3. Activate hand/finger chakras and invocation for self, (Covered in Section-2) Hand: Press firmly into the palm of your right hand using your left thumb. Press in and hold for about two seconds. Do the same with your left hand and right thumb. Stretch arms and feel your tendons

stretch. Fingers: Firmly pinch each fingertip pad with the opposite hand. Then open and close your hand vigorously about ten times.

4. Cleanse your own aura/room, (Covered in Section-2) Aura: Sweep your cupped, dominant hand (palm in) from head to root about five times. Room: You can use sage or incense, carefully; or if you prefer a non smoke method using a blend of essential oils. You may also use visualization of a cleansing, bright, white or green light.

5. Invocation for client, (Covered in Section-2) Hold your hands out, palms up and open. Say the following: "I call upon the Holy Mother, Holy Father, and all healing angels to guide and assist me in the highest healing possible for (insert name of client). Please let the Reiki flow. Please let the Reiki flow. Please let the Reiki flow."

6. Breathing for energy flow, (Covered in Section-2) Breathing in for a count of six, visualize the energy coming down from the crown chakra flowing towards your heart chakra. The energy coming up from your feet chakras is heading towards your heart chakra as well. Upon holding for a count of three the energy reaches and enters your heart chakra. Breathing out for a count of six moves the energy from your heart chakra down your arms and out your hand chakras.

7. Cleanse/Scan client aura and begin front chakras, (Covered in Section-3) Use your dominant hand to sweep your clients aura from head to toe at least five times. Moving at a steady pace with hand cupped slightly, you are scooping away anything that shouldn't be there. Use your intuition to then scan for any odd sensations your hands

feel. Make a note of these locations to go back to after the chakras are done. Place your hand over each chakra for 3-5 minutes.

8. Address any issue that came up during the scan, and finish remaining hand positions, (Covered in Section-3) Those areas you picked up on during the scan should be treated now. Then move on to the hand position (diagrams) for 3-5 minutes each.

9. Turn client over, scan, finish chakras, then remaining hand positions. (Covered in Section-3) Cleanse their backside aura, scan for problem areas, finish backside chakras, then finish up with the hand positions (diagrams) and treat any areas you noted with the scan. Now you may end the session.

ENDING THE SESSION

Ending the session consists of balancing your clients energy and giving thanks for the assistance and guidance you received. We performed the invocation, asking for permission to be a divine conduit or channel for the Reiki to flow through us. Now we balance that energy and give thanks.

To balance your clients energy, place your left hand on their crown chakra (about an inch above the crown of their head) and then place your right hand over their Root or Basic chakra. Hold this position while watching your clients body 3-5 minutes. Any movement from them, even a twitch will signify the balancing is complete. At this time you may give thanks to the divine. Resume the

Gassho position and internally give gratitude for the assistance, guidance, and flow, then bow.

Once you have balanced your client's energy and given thanks to the divine. You may assist your client from their position on the table, so they are upright. Inform your client again of the possible interactions, and ask them how they are feeling. Also, remind them they will enjoy the benefits of their session for a couple more days. They should notice continued improvement and should stay well hydrated to flush out any toxins that the treatment brought to the surface. Many clients can be light-headed, be sure to assist them to a seated position until they normalize.

QUICK TREATMENT OPTIONS

Sometimes life does not allow for a full Reiki treatment. In these cases, when we are away from our usual treatment sight, or our clients only have 15 minutes, there are techniques that we  can perform in these condensed time frames. The plan would be to treat the main chakras first. This includes all the chakras in the head, the heart chakra, solar plexus chakra, sacral or navel chakra, and the root or sex chakra. Spending two minutes on each of these seven chakras leaves you one minute to scan and cleanse their aura.

GROUP TREATMENT OPTIONS

Group treatment options are an excellent way to really

boost your client's immune system. To perform a group treatment, decide in advance what hand positions each person involved will be responsible for. The person at the head will lead the treatment. The leader speaks the invocation, cleanses the aura and balances their energies at the end of the treatment. This method is very powerful and the person receiving has taken in a full Reiki treatment in about 12 to 15 minutes. Multiple group treatments are very useful for those clients suffering from very serious illnesses. It is a good idea to network in class and develop a call list for these occasions. We will have a group session in class if time allows.

This concludes Section 3 of this manual. The section to follow will be about the various uses of Reiki and who or what can benefit. Reiki can literally be used on anything, as you will soon see.

SECTION 4

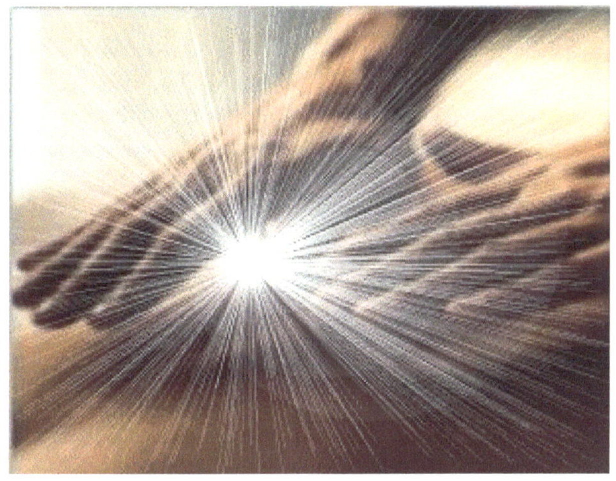

REIKI FOR EVERYTHING
REIKI AND PREGNANCY/BABIES

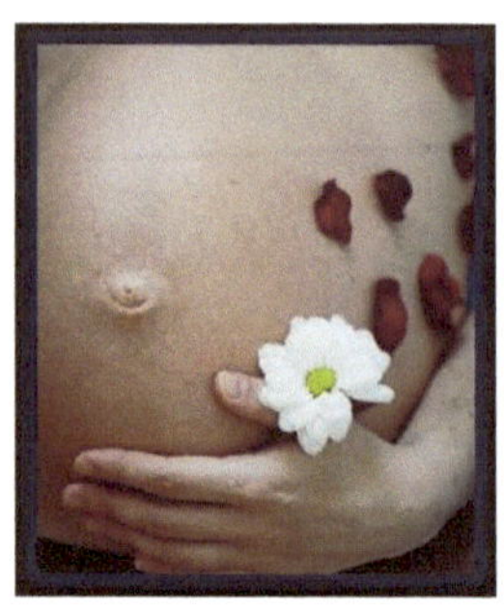

There are amazing benefits for pregnant woman to use Reiki on a daily basis. Many women state their entire pregnancy was more bearable including labor and delivery. When a mother is attuned to Reiki, she passes pure, unconditional love to her baby just by placing her hands on her baby bump! Baby's chakras are in the same place as adults! Here are some of the ways Reiki can help during pregnancy. The benefits are not limited to just this list. New benefits are discovered every day! Always use your intuition!

~Alleviate morning sickness

~Reduce fatigue

~Increases healthy development of the fetus/baby

~Increases the mother/baby bond (when the mother is attuned)

~Increases the father/baby bond (when the father is attuned)

~Decreases the likelihood of postpartum depression or it's significantly reduced

~Reduces stress and stimulates the reproductive cycles of both mother and father when trying to conceive a child.

~Reduces recovery time after delivery; especially cesarean section births, healing stiches, staples, and will even lessen stretch marks by improving skin elasticity.

There are also many benefits specific to baby:

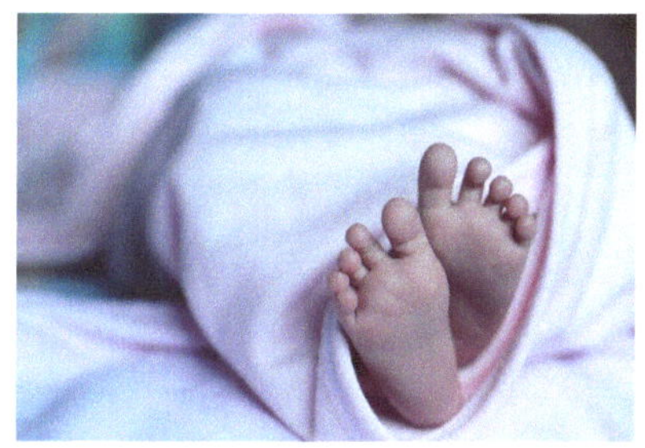

~Calm and sooth after the shock of delivery

~Heal the umbilical cord faster

~Attuned mother can infuse her breast milk with Reiki – in bottle or breast! Formula can be infused as well. This Reiki infusion helps to nourish and satisfy the baby so sleep is better and longer. Helps them suckle longer so they are taking in enough nourishment at feeding time before falling asleep.

~Treat cradle cap, colic, gas, and infuse baby's bath water. The possibilities are only limited by your imagination!

REIKI & CHILDREN

Children can be treated just like adults. The bonus is they are usually more receptive to the energy than us adults! Children are made up of pure unconditional loving energy, they absorb it as easily as it

flows through them. Specifically, children can also be attuned to level I and older children to level II. They are phenomenal with so much love in their little hearts.

Instinctively, we touch or kiss the boo-boos of our children with of hopes of easing their pain. That comes from pure love. That is the essential powering factor behind Reiki energy. Utilizing Reiki can speed healing and boost a child's natural healing or immune system keeping them healthier on a regular basis. Less sickness during cold and flu season is an exciting thought!

Treating and/or attuning your children to Reiki can help them fall asleep and rest better, be better focused students, and it evens out their temperament—less bouts of impulsive or overactive behaviors.
Examples for children (besides a full hands-on treatment) include but are not limited to:

1. Infuse all products the child uses, i.e.,soaps, shampoos, regular medications, supplements, bathwater, etc.
2. Infuse all foods and beverages, i.e., their school lunch for a productive afternoon!
3. Treat behaviors with Reiki by placing one hand on their Crown chakra and the other on Solar Plexus chakra. Especially when they have just injured themselves or heard disturbing news. This balances emotional behaviors. (Use Crown and Root/Basic to balance all energies for better days at school.) Trust me when I tell you their teachers will thank you!

REIKI AND ANIMALS

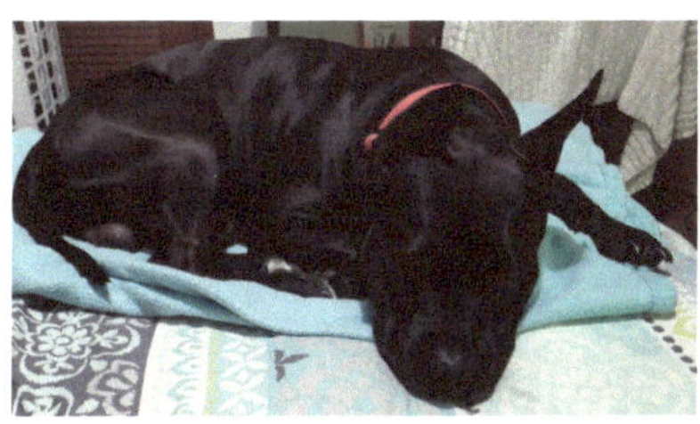

Another beautiful aspect of Reiki energy is we can treat our furry family as well. Meet my Thor! In this photo, notice his healthy, shiny coat. He is totally at peace and resting after his daily treatment. He is so much calmer with an even temperment. If your fur babies are as important to you as mine are to me, this section will really interest you. On the next page is a diagram of the chakra locations in a dog. You can use this diagram as a guide for all animals. Animals will often help you find the location of their illness or injury. My dog rolls over on his back usually to treat his digestive issues. Always follow your intuition. If the

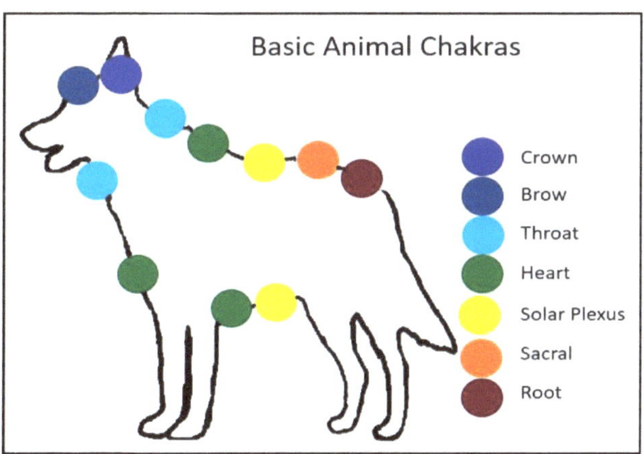

animal moves away at the moment you begin to send reiki, it is likely they are startled as they were not expecting that sensation. Don't give up yet. Let your second attempt be a no touch method or you may have to tone down your energy in the beginning by putting distance between you and the animal. This method works well for unknown animals or those that are perceived as dangerous. The distance method is learned in level II. Treating their food, water, and medications are also beneficial.

REIKI & PLANTS

You can treat your houseplants, your entire garden— everything you grow and care for. When planting anything from seeds or bulbs, simply hold them in your hands for about five minutes and let the Reiki flow. For existing house plants or flower beds, immerse your

fingertips into the soil for about five minutes and let the Reiki flow. Similarly you can gently touch the base of the plant and a few leaves for a few minutes—letting the Reiki flow. A very fun experiment to do with your kids is to plant some seedlings that have been held for five minutes in specially marked cups. Then plant a few others without Reiki and compare the growth of your green babies. You will notice a marked difference and so will your children!

Tree hugging is a real thing. To send large trees the appropriate amount of Reiki, a nice long hug—letting the Reiki flow will do the trick. Repeat this several times a week if the tree has been weakened by disease. You can extend the life of fresh cut flowers in a vase by holding the end of the stems in your hand for three to five minutes and treating their water by immersing your finger tips inside. Similarly, you can treat entire gardens and lawns by treating their water supply. Most people attach a food dispenser to their hose, that is where you would send Reiki.

Level II Reiki covers distance healing. You can help with wild fires, endangered forests, or even areas of famine with poor crops. Developing a group of Reiki friends is powerful healing for all situations. If you can imagine it, you can send it Reiki! Let's change the world together!

REIKI & FOOD/BEVERAGES

In the healthcare industry, the importance of digestion is stressed repeatedly. As well as how much energy the body needs to devote to the process. When we treat our food before we consume it, we are lessoning the work our body has to do, freeing up this vital energy for other systems. You can treat the food as you prepare it, or treat the finished product on your plate if you are at a restaurant.

Lovingly preparing meals for the family takes on a whole new meaning when you infuse all their meals with life force energy! All you need to do is place your seasonings in your hand for about couple minutes and add them to the dish. You can treat the veggies as you chop them or after their chopped by holding them in your hand for a few minutes– with the specific intention of letting the Reiki flow. I enjoy cooking so much more now! When it comes to your beverages, if you don't want to immerse your finger tips, simply hold the container it's in for one to three minutes.

The uses for Reiki really are countless. You can send Reiki to everything in your bathroom, including your medicine cabinet. These are all methods to increase yours and your loved one's life force energy for better living. People who utilize Reiki are genuinely happier and satisfied overall then people who don't.
Reiki creates more positive atmospheres and more positive people. The world needs this! In level II you are given special symbols that boost your Reiki even further and the uses expand to protection and manifesting good fortune to name only two!

TRANSITIONAL REIKI

I used to have a huge problem with death. I have lost several dear family members and I never really learned to cope with death. I used to say, "Death is too hard on the living." I meant that sincerely. Since my studies, I'm a firm believer that we, our souls, live on.

There is so much research today on those people who have experienced death and returned to tell their story. Every single person mentions the feelings of overwhelming peace and love. They mention they know they're dead. All of these people also mention the light in some shape or form as well as a guide to a new plane of existence. Some religious organizations preach fire and brimstone for those who don't behave so-to-speak. But I'm of the belief that we are here to learn, grow, even remember our past mistakes so as to not make them again and again. Eastern philosophies are rich in these beliefs. I recommend you meditate on the subject and go with what resonates with you. For me the evidence is overwhelming, and it resonates deeply. With that we discuss how to help those who are about to lose a loved one, and even helping that special loved one to transition with ease and comfort.

When I lost my father in 2018, I was able to assist the hospice organization and we kept him comfortable. Hours before his death, I had spoke to my father as if he could hear me. I forgave him, and I said I hope he had forgiven

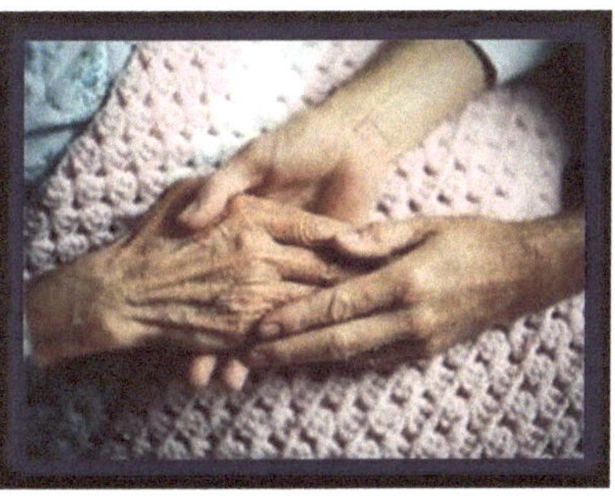

me and most importantly that it's okay to go. Then I asked his angels to guide him to his higher soul. Before I left I even kidded with him and said, no smoking in your next life pops! I believe he left so quickly after that because of my helpful words and prayers to his angels to guide him. I saw the orbs around him, I know they were there. It was truly beautiful. The Reiki that was flowing to him helped to facilitate his transition by keeping him calm and peaceful—without fear.

If you are assisting with a transition. There are several things you can do to be of service, the following list is not exhaustive; use your intuition always.

1. Treat the person transitioning with a steady flow of Reiki the closer they get to their final hour.
2. Treat the family members with Reiki in between the transitioning person.
3. Encourage the family members to speak to the person

(whether they are conscious or not) and resolve any old wounds by offering and asking for forgiveness. Even if you can't recall anything specific, if there is a slight chance the person could be holding on to something, this is very helpful.

4. Encourage the family members to reassure their loved one that it's okay to go. That everyone will be just fine.

5. If you are aware of the final hour approaching, use your invocation or a form of it, to ask that person's angels to guide them on their journey. Wish them safe travels with much love and peace. If you are not sure when their time will come, do it before you leave them for the last time.

6. If the person transitioning is especially fearful, reassure them their soul lives on. Explain we are all energy. Energy never dies; we only leave the body housing our soul-our holy vessel.

DISCLAIMER

Please be advised that Reiki is not to be used instead of valuable medical care. If you are under a doctor's care, be sure to consult him/her before you make any changes to medications, etc. Reiki will make you feel so much better, but have your doctor run tests before you stop taking medicines for blood pressure, diabetes, hypo/hyperthyroidism, etc.; this is very important. Even certain pain medications must be reduced slowly and not stopped abruptly. Reiki compliments western medicine beautifully when it comes to serious conditions. As mentioned earlier, never treat a person with a pacemaker, it can throw off the rhythm. Similarly, if you treat someone with diabetes, advise them to test their glucose before each anticipated, regular dose. Reiki lessons the need for insulin.

YOUR FUTURE IN REIKI

Congratulations! You have completed Progressive Usui Reiki, Level I. I encourage you to continue your studies by completing Level II as well. There are many benefits to being certified at Level II. Your knowledge will expand to different types of treatments, you will learn the importance of Reiki symbols and how to use them properly, as well as how to treat your clients from a distance. These are all very valuable tools to have.

Practice, practice, practice! The more you let your Reiki flow, the more it flows freely and easily. You may email me should you ever have any questions along your path. energyforwellnessinyou@gmail.com.

See you in level II!

Stay Tuned For More Works By

Tammie L. Hada